HOCKEY HEROES

Dominik Hasek

SEAN ROSSITER

Special research in the Czech Republic
by Peter Buchar Sr. and Jr.

GREYSTONE BOOKS
Douglas & McIntyre
Vancouver/Toronto/New York

Greystone Books
A division of Douglas & McIntyre Ltd.
2323 Quebec Street, Suite 201
Vancouver, British Columbia
Canada V5T 4S7

Canadian Cataloguing in Publication Data
Rossiter, Sean—
    Dominik Hasek
    (Hockey heroes)
    ISBN 1-55054-679-1
    1. Hasek, Dominik—Juvenile literature. 2. Hockey goalkeepers—
Biography—Juvenile literature. I. Title. II. Series: Hockey heroes
(Vancouver, B.C.).
GV848.5.H38R67 1999   j796.962′092   C99-910171-4

Editing by Michael Carroll
Cover and text design by Peter Cocking
Front cover photograph by John Giamundo/Bruce Bennett Studios
Back cover photograph by Mike Corrado/Bruce Bennett Studios
Printed and bound in Canada by Friesens on acid-free paper ∞

Every reasonable care has been taken to trace the ownership of copyrighted
visual material. Information that will enable the publisher to rectify any
reference or credit is welcome.

All NHL logos and marks and team logos and marks depicted herein are the
property of the NHL and the respective teams and may not be reproduced
without the prior written consent of NHL Enterprises, Inc. © 1999 NHL.

The publisher gratefully acknowledges the assistance of the Canada Council
for the Arts and of the British Columbia Ministry of Tourism, Small
Business and Culture. The publisher also acknowledges the financial
support of the Government of Canada through the Book Publishing Industry
Development Program for its publishing activities.

Canada

Photo credits

Photos by Bruce Bennett Studios:
pp. i (top and bottom), 12, 20, 23,
31, 35, 36, 39, 40, 43: Bruce Bennett
pp. i (center left), 24, 27:
Richard Lewis
pp. i (center right), iii, 4, 7,
11, 16, 28: Jim McIsaac
p. 8: Andre Pichette
p. 32: Jim Leary

Photos by CTK:
p. iv: Jan Trestik
p. 3: Alexandra Mlejnkova
p. 15: Libor Hajsky
p. 17: Zdenek Havelka
p. 19: Michal Dolezal

CONTENTS

Dominik says winning the gold medal in the 1998. Olympics in Japan was the best hockey moment in his entire life.

A Hero Returns

After each National Hockey League season, Dominik "The Dominator" Hasek returns home to the Czech Republic. As great as the Buffalo Sabres goalie has played, most summers his return is a quiet one. But during the summer of 1998, Dominik returned to find 7,000 of his neighbors cheering him in the town square of Pardubice (pronounced Par-du-bee-tsuh).

June 29, 1998, was a beautiful, moonlit night. William Nack of *Sports Illustrated* magazine wrote in his article "A Prague Summer" that here and there in the crowd gathered in the 600-year-old square of Dominik's hometown were signs that said, in the Czech language, "Hasek Is God! Hasek Is God!"

Dominik knew better. But what could he say?

Over the loudspeaker, rock music was playing. "We are the champions," the song went. "We are the champions—of the world..."

That is how every Czech had felt since February—like a world champion. When the Czech national team won the Olympic gold medal in hockey at Nagano, Japan, it was the greatest thing to happen since the people overthrew their Communist rulers in 1989 and the Czech Republic became a separate country on January 1, 1993. Defeating Russia, the Czechs' old masters, in the final game only made it better.

The Dominator's fans in Pardubice love their favorite goalie.

Dominik stood on a stage built just for that night. He waved to the hometown crowd with his right hand, holding a teddy bear in his left. He looked uneasy.

Then the music stopped, and the crowd began chanting "Dominik! Dominik! Dominik!"

How does a national hero answer people who chant his name and carry signs calling him God?

He says thank you.

"It's absolutely wonderful what you have done for me," Dominik told the crowd. "I can't explain the way I feel. I'm very happy that we could win the gold medal for our country. It was the best hockey moment in my entire life."

If some Czechs wanted to honor the key player on their national team by calling him God, maybe they were only getting a little carried away. The 33-year-old who waved to his friends and neighbors that June night had just finished one of the most amazing seasons any athlete has ever had.

There was the Olympic gold medal. There was Dominik's second consecutive Hart Trophy as the NHL's most valuable player. He was the first goalie ever to win the Hart twice. He had also won the Vezina Trophy as the NHL's top goaltender for the fourth time in five years.

But Dominik's great season had a rocky start. The trouble began at the end of the previous season, 1996–97, which had been an okay one for Dominik. He was the first goalie in 35 years to be the National Hockey League MVP, and he won his third Vezina.

USE IT, DON'T LOSE IT

Twenty years ago most goalies wore head protection like Dominik Hasek's. Today, only a handful of NHL goalies wear the helmet-and-cage style of headgear. They include the Dominator, the Carolina Hurricane's Arturs Irbe and the Detroit Red Wings' Stanley Cup-winning goaltender, Chris Osgood. All the rest wear molded fiberglass masks.

Helmets have more padding, so their hard shells are farther from the head. That leaves more room to absorb shocks. A wire cage mounted on a helmet sits farther away from the face than the same cage mounted on a tight fiberglass mask.

Better protection is one reason Dominik allows his team to shoot at his head in practice. In fact, he asks them to do it. He uses his headgear like any other piece of goaltending equipment—to stop shots and direct rebounds into the corners.

No other goalie uses his head that way. No goalie is less likely to lose it, either.

In the playoffs, though, everything came apart. Somehow the goalie who has won more NHL awards than any player since Wayne Gretzky was being blasted for not wanting to win. He was being called a quitter!

Going into the 1997 playoffs, Dominik and Buffalo's coach, Ted Nolan, weren't happy with each other. Dominik felt the coach was blaming him for the team's problems.

Then, on April 21, 1997, early in the third playoff game with the Ottawa Senators, Dominik was down on the ice with his knees together and his feet spread so his pads covered most of the goalmouth ice. This is called the butterfly position because a goalie's pads are spread like the wings of a butterfly. In this position, a goaltender has the lower net covered but is helpless to avoid contact. One of the Senators' forwards, Sergei Zoltok, crashed into him.

Dominik didn't see Zoltok coming. As the Ottawa player fell on him, Dominik felt part of his right knee crack. He knew right away it was serious—the worst knee injury he had ever suffered. He thought he would be out of action for a month.

Dominik's first mistake was to tell reporters the truth: he was hurt. You aren't supposed to do that during the playoffs.

Dominik's Secrets

The keys to Dominik Hasek's goaltending style are flexibility, the way his hands and eyes work together, and the quickest feet in the NHL. Dominik stretches all the time, not just before games. He can even do the splits. As a former teenage tennis champion, he sees shots right into his gloves. His biggest secret? Author Bruce Dowbiggin writes that Dominik played both soccer and "a Czech game called nohy ball—a combination of soccer and volleyball—in which you kick a ball over a net about a meter high. The results are obvious."

After the game, he had dinner with his childhood pal, Frank Musil, then a member of the Senators. There he was, hanging out with a player from the other team!

Things got worse when Dominik decided to stand behind the Buffalo bench during the next game. How could he do that with a bad knee?

Then Jim Kelley, a sports columnist, wrote that he had seen Dominik run to his vehicle in the Buffalo arena parking lot. When he saw the columnist near the Sabres' dressing room, Dominik lost his temper, grabbed the newspaperman by the throat and backed him against the wall.

Dominik apologized the next day, but the NHL suspended him for three games. The Sabres lost the playoff series. The team's general manager, John Muckler, was fired in May, and Nolan, their popular coach, decided not to accept the contract the team offered him.

Buffalo fans blamed Dominik. They booed him when his name was announced before home games as the 1997–98 season began. His goals-against average (GAA)—the average number of goals allowed by a goalie per game—went up by one goal in Buffalo's first 20 games. *Sports Illustrated* said he had gone "from MVP to MDP (most disappointing player)."

Fellow Czech Martin Rucinsky tests the Dominator.

The turning point in Dominik's season may have been a 3–2 loss to the New Jersey Devils on November 22. In that game, the Devils' Doug Gilmour scored on a breakaway in the first period. Before the game was half finished he had given up three goals. Then he blanked New Jersey through the last 35 minutes. In the next month, December, he had six shutouts, tying the NHL record for most shutouts in a month.

Going into the Winter Olympics in February 1998, Dominik was the hottest goaltender in the NHL. The Sabres were undefeated in nine games. The Olympics gave Dominik a global stage on television, a place to show everyone he was the best in the world at his position.

And what about that teddy bear in Pardubice? It was one of a dozen or so tossed onstage by teenage girls, each with a note attached. One note wished him good luck in the Stanley Cup playoffs.

Those good wishes were a little late. The Buffalo Sabres had lost in the third round of the NHL playoffs to the Washington Capitals in six games. But that was the best performance by the Sabres in the playoffs since 1979–80. Just before his return to Pardubice, Dominik signed a new four-year contract that would pay him $7 million per season.

THE DOMINIK HASEK FILE

Position: Goaltender

Born: January 29, 1965, Pardubice, Czech Republic

Height: Five feet eleven inches (1.8 meters)

Weight: 165 pounds (76.2 kilograms)

Catches: Left

Number: 39

Nickname: The Dominator

Favorite Food: Czech dumplings made with pork and cabbage

Favorite Book: *The Three Musketeers*

Hobby: Chess

Childhood Sports Hero: Tennis champion Bjorn Borg

Hockey Highlight: Gold medal, 1998 Winter Olympics

Dominik doesn't really have an idol, nor did he copy one style. He learned his craft by studying every goalie.

CHAPTER TWO

Growing Up Czech

t was no big deal for Dominik Hasek when he was drafted by the Chicago Blackhawks in 1983. He was 18. He had already played two seasons in the Czech First Division, the highest level in his country. He was invited to try out for the national team.

Dominik was the 11th choice of the Blackhawks, the 199th player selected overall. Other players drafted in 1983 were Pat LaFontaine, Steve Yzerman, Tom Barrasso, Cam Neely and Frank Musil. The flood of European players into the NHL was just beginning.

In Canada or the United States, a player drafted by a pro team is big news. Believe it or not, Dominik didn't even find out about being drafted for a couple of months.

"I didn't care. It made no difference to me," he told Stan Fischler, author of *Goalies: Legends from the NHL's Toughest Job.*

Dominik was born in Pardubice, Czechoslovakia, on January 29, 1965. His father, Jan, was a uranium miner and amateur soccer player. His mother, Marie, played tennis when she was young. His grandfather, Anthony Tyrl, took young Dominik to hockey games at the Pardubice arena. Dominik was so crazy about the home team that his granddad carried extra handkerchiefs to soak up his tears when they lost.

Dominik loved to compete from the very beginning. Most goaltenders start out at another position. Not Dominik. In soccer or hockey, he was always a goalie.

Dominik was upset after losing the 1987 World Cup.

He played for fun on a nearby pond with friends or defended the kitchen door of the Hasek household against his father and grandfather. Jan Hasek made the six-year-old Dominik a pair of skates by attaching blades to a pair of boots.

There were between 200 and 300 six-year-olds who wanted to play hockey in Pardubice in the fall of 1971, but there were only 40 openings. Dominik was already good enough to play with eight-year-olds. In time, the Pardubice youth teams Dominik backstopped became the best in Czechoslovakia. They won all the tournaments. One season they lost only one game.

THE NINES HAVE IT

Number 9 has always been a special number for hockey players. It was the number Maurice Richard, Gordie Howe and Bobby Hull wore. Paul Kariya wears number 9. Wayne Gretzky wears 99 only because 9 was already taken when he joined his junior team.

As a five-time goalie of the year and three-time player of the year in Czech hockey, Dominik Hasek earned the right to wear any number he wanted. He chose 9.

But there are rules about numbers in the NHL. Goalies can wear many numbers, but not 9. When Dominik arrived in Chicago, he was issued Number 31. Later, he asked for another number that ended in 9. The obvious one was 29, but Greg Millen, an NHL veteran, already had that number.

So Dominik went with the next number that ends in 9. And that's why he's the first goalie in the NHL ever to wear 39.

Like most young goalies, Dominik coached himself. In Chris McDonell's *For the Love of Hockey: Hockey Stars' Personal Stories*, he says: "The only advice I got was to keep my stick on the ice, watch the puck and make the save. I learned by watching every goalie I could find.... I didn't have an idol or try to copy one particular goalie; I studied them all."

By the time Dominik's younger brother, Martin, was able to move around, the two were playing tennis in their bedroom. Dominik was good enough as a tennis player to become junior champion of his region in the former Czechoslovakia. His favorite athlete was the Swedish tennis champion Bjorn Borg. Today Martin is a soccer player with Sparta Prague, the 1997 Czech professional champions.

At 16, Dominik had fulfilled his dream: to play goal for his city's team in Czechoslovakia's First Division. His first game was a 5–1 victory over Zlin in November 1981. He regrets that single goal to this day. By 1984, when he was 19, he was playing for his country in the Canada Cup.

"I started thinking about the NHL back in 1984," Dominik told Bruce Dowbiggin, author of *Of Ice and Men*. "Someone said you can make $150,000 a year and get a big BMW car just for signing. But before the revolution"—when Czechoslovakia rid itself of Communist rule in 1989—"if you leave the country, you can't go back. You leave your parents and everything behind."

Chicago scouts stayed in touch. By 1987, Dominik was not only the national team goaltender but had won the First Division championship with Pardubice. Bob Pulford, the Chicago general manager, met Dominik in Vienna at the 1987 World Championships and told him that if he signed with Chicago, he would be the third-highest-paid player on the team.

"I turned him down because I was very happy where I was," Dominik says in *For the Love of Hockey*. "I was single and I had enough money—I could buy what I wanted, I had a car... I was also attending university and wanted to graduate."

Dominik and the Pardubice team won a second Czechoslovak league championship in 1989. He was drafted again—this time by an organization that made him an offer he couldn't refuse—the Czechoslovak army. He joined the army's powerhouse hockey club, Dukla Jihlava, for the 1989–90 season, and recorded a very impressive 2.13, the lowest GAA of his nine-year career in Czechoslovak hockey.

The Soviets score on Dominik in a 1987 exhibition game.

"By 1989, I had my degree and was married," Dominik explains in *For the Love of Hockey*. "I thought more about the NHL and decided to try it. It was a tough transition, because in Czechoslovakia I was a pretty big star."

When Dominik came to North America, he had a college degree in education. He could speak three languages: Czech, Russian and English. At 25, he was already a success in life and a hero in his hometown of Pardubice.

None of this meant anything to the NHL.

Dominik was playing at a

level that placed him

among the top five goalies

in the NHL. And nobody

knew who he was.

C H A P T E R   T H R E E

Off to America

For most people, history is something that happens to others. But after Czechoslovakia became free in 1989, Dominik was allowed to go to North America and play in the NHL when he chose to.

He arrived in Edmonton the summer of 1990 to work out with NHL players. Then he attended his first NHL training camp with the Chicago Blackhawks that fall.

During the telecast of a scoreless tie between Buffalo and the New York Rangers, Craig Simpson, who scored 56 goals with Pittsburgh and Edmonton in 1987–88, remembered Dominik in those scrimmages during the summer of 1990. "He was just over from the Czech Republic. He had all new equipment, and he looked like he'd won a contest to be a Goalie for a Day. His pads looked like twin beds."

In 1990–91, the Chicago Blackhawks were on the rise. The season before, the team had improved more than any other club in the NHL. The improvement was due to the club's new coach, "Iron Mike" Keenan.

Goalie Ed Belfour had played some games for Chicago in each of the past two seasons, but in 1990–91 he played 74 games (the most of any NHL goalie), won 43 (also the most in the league) and posted a 2.47 GAA (the lowest). Belfour won the Calder Trophy as the NHL's top rookie and the Vezina Trophy as the top goalie. He also made the first All-Star team.

There wasn't much room for Dominik or any goalie other than Belfour with the Blackhawks that year. Dominik thought he earned a place with the big club at training camp. Perhaps he did. He did play parts of five games for the Blackhawks, winning three (losing none) and recording a fine 2.46 GAA.

Dominik's first sweater number with Chicago was 31.

But Dominik spent most of his first season in North America in the minor leagues. He played 33 games with Chicago's International Hockey League farm club at Indianapolis, leading that league in shutouts, with four, and GAA, at 2.52. Dominik was also the IHL's first-team all-star goaltender.

His second season in the Chicago system was a step upward. He tended goal in 20 games each at Chicago and Indianapolis in 1991–92, playing much better in the NHL. With Chicago he won 10 games and posted a GAA of 2.60.

Ed Belfour was again one of the top NHL goalies, playing 52 games with a 2.70 GAA and leading the league with five shutouts. Another goalie, Jimmy Waite, played in 17 games, winning four and losing seven, with a 3.69 GAA.

Dominik was a better goalie than Waite in 1991–92. He made the NHL/Upper Deck All-Rookie team for 1992. But he left a lasting impression when the Blackhawks went all the way to the Stanley Cup finals against the Pittsburgh Penguins.

The Penguins swept the final series in four games. Keenan replaced Belfour with Dominik for the second half of Game 4.

Harry Neale, who covered that game for *Hockey Night in Canada*, saw Dominik shut out the great Mario Lemieux one-on-one three times in 30 minutes. But Neale says nobody thought much about what they had seen because Pittsburgh was leading at the time. They figured Lemieux wasn't really trying to score.

At the end of the 1991–92 season, Dominik told author Bruce

Dowbiggin: "Mike Keenan called me and said that Jimmy Waite had the starting job. I began to think maybe I wasn't so good. I told Keenan I didn't want to stay."

Looking back, Dominik says he learned by playing in the minor leagues. "I had to learn to play with my stick. In Czechoslovakia, the goalie never went behind the net or into the corner. That was considered the job of the defense," he explained to Chris McDonell in *For the Love of Hockey*.

Dominik hated playing in the minors and thought about ending his NHL career. But he was about to turn the corner toward NHL stardom. On August 7, 1992, six weeks after the 1991–92 season ended, Dominik was traded by Mike Keenan to the Buffalo Sabres.

The Sabres, like Chicago, were a team that was getting better. When Dominik came to Buffalo that summer, the other goalies were Daren Puppa, who had been with the Sabres for eight years, and Tom Draper.

In February 1993, halfway through the season, Buffalo traded Puppa (and high-scorer Dave Andreychuk) for Grant Fuhr. Dominik would have to compete with Fuhr, who had won four Stanley Cups with the Edmonton Oilers in the 1980s.

Velvet Revolution

Not every NHL player can claim that his career in professional hockey was affected by world events. Dominik Hasek was Czechoslovak goalie of the year for five straight seasons ending in 1989–90 with the country's army team, but he wasn't free to join the NHL until early in his last season.

On November 17, 1989, the Communist government fell in Prague, Czechoslovakia's capital. Against orders, Dominik and four teammates drove to Prague to see history being made. Czechoslovakia's freedom became his freedom.

In 1992–93, Dominik's first season with Buffalo, the games were shared among four goaltenders: Fuhr (29), Dominik (28), Puppa (24) and Draper (11). But Dominik had the best GAA: 3.15 to Fuhr's 3.47.

By then, Dominik had been playing in the NHL for parts of three seasons. He had played in 53 NHL regular-season games for a total of 2,638 minutes with Chicago and Buffalo, giving up 129 goals for a 2.89 GAA.

How many NHL goalies who played 40 games or more in 1992–93 had GAAs below three? Two: Felix Potvin of Toronto (2.50) and Ed Belfour of Chicago (2.70). Dominik Hasek was playing at a level that placed him among the top five goaltenders in the NHL.

And hardly anyone outside Buffalo knew who he was.

HOCKEY'S KRAMER

Dominik Hasek is known as "Kramer" to his Buffalo Sabres teammates for his habit of bursting into team meetings at the last possible moment. He even looks a bit like the character in the popular television show, *Seinfeld*. Like Kramer, Dominik is also forgetful, often sleeps in and has been known to show up late.

Frank Musil of the Edmonton Oilers, who played with Dominik in the former Czechoslovakia, tells a typical story. Five minutes before the team arrived for a game in another town, Dominik announced that he had forgotten his goalie pads. Playing with borrowed pads, the Dominator backstopped his Pardubice team to a 2–1 win and was the first star.

It's a good thing for Dominik that, in the NHL, the team takes care of things like his goalie pads. He now arrives in the Sabres' dressing room for home games two hours before the faceoff. That way he can have a cup of coffee, stretch and put on his equipment—all before the warm-up.

In 1993–94, Dominik

stopped more of the shots

he faced than any other

goalie and led the NHL in

save percentage with .930.

CHAPTER FOUR

The Dominator

Dominik began 1993–94 as Grant Fuhr's backup. But early that season Fuhr was injured. This was Dominik's chance, and he had a brilliant season from start to finish. Now the hockey world had to take note. It no longer mattered *how* he played, because he was playing so well.

"People say that I flop around on the ice like some kind of fish," Dominik explains in *Sports Illustrated for Kids*. "I say 'Who cares, as long as I stop the puck?'"

Dominik played 58 games that year, recording a 1.95 GAA—the first average below two in the NHL in 20 years. Bernie Parent did it in 1973–74 for the Philadelphia Flyers. But the 1994 Sabres weren't nearly as good as the Stanley Cup-winning Flyers of 1974, even if they did improve as a team for the third straight year, finishing the regular season with 95 points. Dominik also led the league in shutouts with seven.

Playing for a fourth-place team in a tough division, Dominik was the key to Buffalo becoming the best defensive team in the NHL that year. The Sabres gave up only 218 goals in 1993–94.

That meant Dominik and Fuhr (who played 32 games with a 3.68 GAA) shared the William M. Jennings Trophy, awarded to the goalies on the least-scored-upon team in the NHL. Dominik also won the Vezina Trophy as the best goalie in the league, and was the first-team All-Star goaltender.

A Better Yardstick

The most common way to rate goalies is by goals-against average (GAA). But a good team can help a goalie lower his or her average. So save percentage is a better method to compare netminders. How does it work? The total number of saves a goalie makes is divided by the number of shots faced, which evens out the differences among teams. Dominik Hasek led the NHL in save percentage in 1993–94 with .930, the highest since the NHL began keeping the statistic. And he has led the NHL in save percentage since.

If winning the Vezina didn't tell the world that Dominik Hasek had arrived, the 1994 playoffs did. Although Buffalo lost its first-round series to New Jersey, the series was pushed to seven games in an unforgettable sixth-game duel between Dominik and the Devils' Martin Brodeur on the night of April 27 and the next morning. The game was a scoreless tie through enough

time for two full games. Dominik stopped 70 shots before the
Sabres' Dave Hannan scored in the fourth overtime period.
It was the sixth-longest game in NHL history.

The 1994–95 season was delayed by a lockout, but aside
from that, it was almost a repeat of the previous one for Dominik. He won the Vezina, was a first-team All-Star, led the league
in save percentage and tied for the league lead in shutouts (five)
and GAA (2.11). That February, Fuhr was traded to Los Angeles.

The following season, 1995–96, Dominik's GAA rose to
2.83—still below three, but high for him—and the Sabres fell
to fifth in their division, failing to make the playoffs. But, with
.920, Dominik still led the NHL in save percentage for the
third straight year. So he was still stopping more of the shots
he faced then any other NHL goalie.

But Dominik became more than just the most effective
goaltender in the NHL in 1996–97. The Buffalo team didn't
seem to be getting any better. Some saw this
edition of the Sabres as the weakest in four years.
Pat LaFontaine, by far the club's highest scorer,
appeared in only 13 games that season.

So the Buffalo Sabres changed. Rallying
around their goaltender, the team's young players
became tight checkers. Captain Mike Peca, in his
second year with the Sabres, won the Frank Selke Trophy as the
best defensive forward in the NHL, and Buffalo finished first in
their division. Their coach, Ted Nolan, won the Jack Adams
Award as NHL coach of the year.

> Dominik deflects
> the puck high into
> the air and away.

Dominik's save percentage returned to .930—the fourth straight year he had led the league in that statistic. And, while he was among the league leaders in GAA (2.27, for fourth place) and wins (37, tied for second with Brodeur), his awards that season showed the respect he had won around the NHL.

The NHL's general managers vote on the Vezina Trophy, and in 1997 they gave it to Dominik for the third time in four years. The Lester B. Pearson Award for the outstanding player in the NHL is voted on by the players. Dominik won that, too, the first goalie to do so since the St. Louis Blues' Mike Liut in 1981. The Hart Trophy, for the NHL's most valuable player, is voted on by hockey writers. They selected Dominik, who was the first goalie to win the award since the Montreal Canadiens' Jacques Plante in 1962 and only the fifth goalie ever to win it since 1924.

Dominik's fellow players, the general managers and the hockey writers were in rare agreement that the Dominator was not only the best goalie in the NHL, but the best player. Period.

MAN WHO WINS AWARDS

Dominik Hasek has won the most awards of any goalie ever to play hockey. In Czechoslovakia he was goaltender of the year five times (1986, 1987, 1988, 1989, 1990); player of the year three times (1987, 1989, 1990); and first-team all-star three times (1988, 1989, 1990).

In the NHL, Dominik has won the Vezina Trophy four times as the top goaltender (1994, 1995, 1997, 1998); the Lester B. Pearson Award twice as the most outstanding player (1997, 1998); the Hart Trophy twice as the most valuable player (1997, 1998); and, with Grant Fuhr, the William M. Jennings Trophy as one of the goalies on the least-scored-upon team (1994). He has also played in NHL All-Star games three times (1996, 1997, 1998).

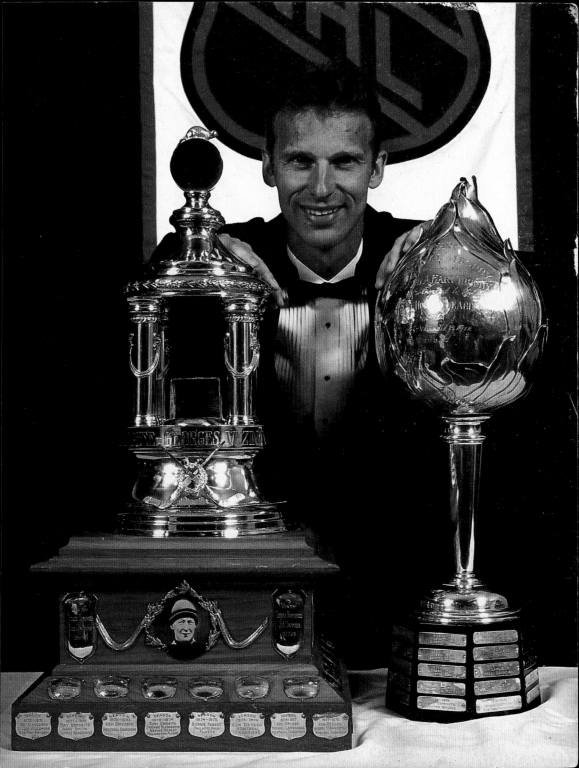

In 1998, Dominik and the

Czechs surprised everyone

by defeating the Russians

and winning Olympic gold

in Nagano, Japan.

The Best in the World

Because his style is so different from other goalies, it took Dominik years to get credit for being as good as he is. In fact, it wasn't until his amazing play in the Winter Olympics at Nagano, Japan, that he proved to everyone he was the best goalie on the planet.

Canada and the Czech Republic met on February 20, 1998, in the Olympic semifinal. Canada was undefeated. The Czechs had lost one game, 2–1 to Russia.

It was a classic. There was no score until the third period when Czech defenseman Jiri Slegr snaked a shot past Patrick

Roy, the Canadian netminder. Even late in the third period, as Canada pressed for the equalizer, it looked as if Canada would never score. Dominik was dominating.

But Trevor Linden did score from a scramble with just over a minute left. His shot deflected off a Czech defenseman's stick and hit where the crossbar and goalpost met to Dominik's left.

Canada outshot the Czechs five to one in the 10-minute overtime, but never came close to scoring. So it came down to the shootout. Dominik stopped all five Canadian shooters. Later, the Czechs defeated Russia for the gold medal.

Being the best one-on-one goalie in hockey was the key to winning the Olympics for Dominik. The Dominator believes that in today's fast-moving game, a goalie has no time to react. A goalie has to be ready before the shot comes.

Dominik's secret is to practice making big saves. That means keeping the puck in play during drills and stopping first, second and sometimes third rebounds. On a third rebound, a goalie's head is often all he has to make that fourth save. So Dominik practices deflecting shots with his headgear.

The best one-on-one goalie in hockey beats Eric Lindros.

"Because I want to stop every puck, I try maybe this weird save in practice," he told Mark Brender of *The Hockey News.* "Of course I like to be faced in the right direction and stop it, but sometimes on rebounds or passes you find yourself out of position. It's a part of the game, so if it happens I try to stop the puck in maybe a weird way, but it is also a way to stop the puck."

Very few goaltenders practice hard. If a player has been scoring on Dominik in practice, he will keep him on the ice until he can stop that player. He once asked Mike Peca to come back out on the ice to take more shots *after* the team captain was in the dressing room and had removed most of his equipment. Peca pulled his cold, wet gear back on and returned to the ice. That's why he is Buffalo's captain.

Hockey scouts know that Dominik's feet, made quick and agile by controlling a soccer ball, are the fastest in hockey. He is very flexible and stretches his muscles every day. He can do the splits to kick out a shot headed for a low corner. More often, he can drop into the butterfly position, filling almost the entire six feet along the ice between the goalposts.

Because Dominik covers the ice so well, shooters think they can score on him by raising the puck over him. But the closer they come, the harder it is to hit the top corners. And the more likely the Dominator will catch the puck.

He uses his blocker—the glove he holds his stick with—like another catching glove. Once the shot is in the air, he sometimes drops his stick to bat the puck away. If he has control of the puck on his right side, he will drop the stick so he can cover the puck with his right hand.

Dominik makes his most amazing saves flat on his back. He knows that a goalie who is down after making a first save is often scored on as he scrambles to get back up. So it's better to stay flat on the ice.

Once, Dominik made a save off the Washington Capitals' Adam Oates in Game 5 of the 1998 playoffs. He was on his back and reached past his head with his blocker just as Oates tried to jam the puck into the opening. That was probably the play that sent the series to a sixth game.

Dominik's great secret is to practice making big saves.

Dominik already ranks among the all-time greats at his position. Only Bill Durnan, Jacques Plante and Ken Dryden have won the Vezina Trophy more times, and all of them played for the Montreal Canadiens, the best club in NHL history.

In one season, 1997–98, Dominik became a hero around the world—in Buffalo, New York, in Nagano, Japan, and in Pardubice, Czech Republic. He would have a star named after him, and a stamp of him was printed to celebrate the Olympic victory.

Dixon Ward, Dominik's Buffalo Sabres teammate, says the Dominator is "the best athlete in any sport. He's better than Michael Jordan is in basketball. He's better than Tiger Woods is in golf."

So what's left for Dominik Hasek? The Stanley Cup, of course. If Dominik and the Buffalo Sabres do win the Cup, what would people call him then? Maybe not God. Maybe something more likely. Perhaps a patron saint of hockey. Why not St. Dominik of the Nets?

OLYMPIC SHOOTOUT

The shootout is one of hockey's most dramatic moments—a showdown between shooter and goalie. At the 1998 Winter Olympics in Nagano, Japan, one of the most thrilling shootouts in history took place.

After 10 minutes of overtime, the semifinal between Canada and the Czech Republic was still tied 1–1. To settle the issue, each team had five breakaway shots. Robert Reichel, the second Czech shooter, scored on Canada's Patrick Roy. At the other end, Dominik stopped four Canadian superstars: Theoren Fleury, Ray Borque, Joe Nieuwendyk and Eric Lindros. Only Brendan Shanahan was left.

Dominik expected him to shoot. "I was talking to myself," he said later. "'Shoot, shoot, you'll hit me and we can go home.'"

Shanahan skated in with the puck ready to shoot. He faked the shot, dropped Dominik to the ice and went to his forehand side. The Dominator's long left leg and catching glove stretched all the way to the left post. The puck hit his pad as it rose from Shanahan's stick.

The Czech underdogs had beaten mighty Canada! The next day Dominik shut out the hated Russians 1–0 for the gold medal.

S T A T I S T I C S

International Hockey League (IHL)

Regular Season

Year	Team	GP	W	L	T	SO	GAA
1990–91	Indianapolis	33	20	11	1	5	2.52
1991–92	Indianapolis	20	7	10	3	1	3.56
Totals		53	27	21	4	6	2.81

Playoffs

Year	Team	GP	W	L	T	SO	GAA
1991	Indianapolis	1	1	0	0	0	3.00

National Hockey League (NHL)

Regular Season

Year	Team	GP	W	L	T	SO	GAA
1990–91	Chicago	5	3	0	1	0	2.46
1991–92	Chicago	20	10	4	1	1	2.60
1992–93	Buffalo	28	11	10	4	0	3.15
1993–94	Buffalo	58	30	20	6	7	1.95
1994–95	Buffalo	41	19	14	7	5	2.11
1995–96	Buffalo	59	22	30	6	2	2.83
1996–97	Buffalo	67	37	20	10	5	2.27
1997–98	Buffalo	72	33	23	13	13	2.09
1998–99	Buffalo	64	30	18	14	9	1.87
Totals		414	195	139	62	42	2.18

Playoffs

Year	Team	GP	W	L	SO	GAA
1991	Chicago	3	0	0	0	2.61
1992	Chicago	3	0	2	0	3.04
1993	Buffalo	1	1	0	0	1.33
1994	Buffalo	7	3	4	2	1.61
1995	Buffalo	5	1	4	0	3.50
1996	Buffalo	Did Not Qualify				
1997	Buffalo	3	1	1	0	1.96
1998	Buffalo	15	10	5	1	2.03
1999	Buffalo	19	13	6	2	1.77
Totals		56	29	22	5	2.06

Czechoslovak/Czech Teams

Year	Team	GP	GAA
1981–82	Pardubice	12	3.09
1982–83	Pardubice	42	2.67
1983–84	Pardubice	40	2.81
1984–85	Pardubice	42	3.25
1985–86	Pardubice	45	3.08
1986–87	Pardubice	43	2.46
1987–88	Pardubice	31	3.00
	Olympics	5	4.98
1988–89	Pardubice	42	2.73
1989–90	Dukla Jihlava	40	2.13
1994–95	Pardubice	2	2.90
1997–98	Olympics	6	0.97

Key

GP = Games Played   W = Wins   L = Losses   T = Ties
SO = Shutouts   GAA = Goals-Against Average